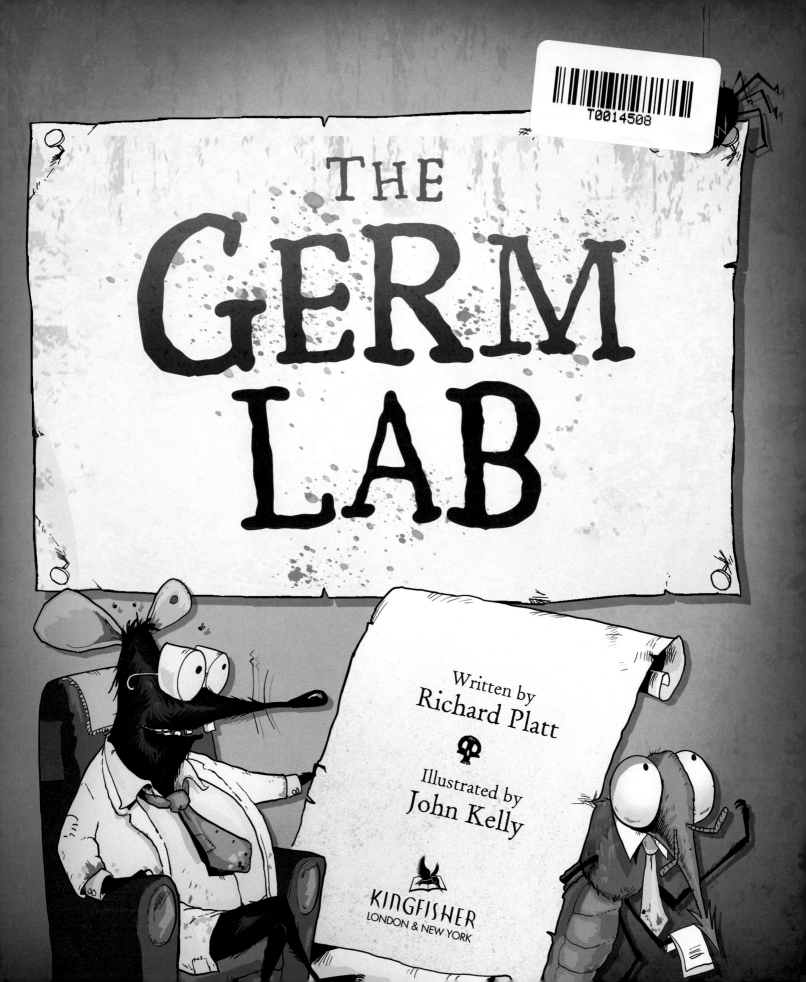

THE GERM LAB

Written by
Richard Platt

Illustrated by
John Kelly

KINGFISHER
LONDON & NEW YORK

T0014508

KINGFISHER
LONDON & NEW YORK

Copyright © Macmillan Publishers
International Ltd 2011, 2020, 2023

Published in the United States by Kingfisher,
120 Broadway, New York, NY 10271
Kingfisher is an imprint of
Macmillan Children's Books, London

Consultant: Selina Hurley, Assistant Curator
of Medicine, Science Museum, London

Concept and Design: Jo Connor

ISBN 978-0-7534-7881-3

Distributed in the U.S. and Canada by Macmillan,
120 Broadway, New York, NY 10271

EU representative: Macmillan Publishers Ireland Ltd,
1st Floor, The Liffey Trust Centre, 117-126 Sheriff Street
Upper, Dublin 1, D01 YC43

Library of Congress Cataloging-in-Publication
Data has been applied for.

Kingfisher books are available for special
promotions and premiums.

For details contact: Special Markets Department,
Macmillan, 120 Broadway, New York, NY 10271

For more information, please visit www.kingfisherbooks.com

Printed in China
1 3 5 7 9 8 6 4 2
1TR/1222/WKT/UNTD/128MA

MIX
Paper | Supporting
responsible forestry
FSC® C116313

CONTENTS

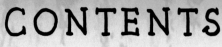

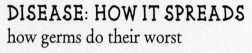
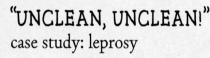

Dr. Scratch
(a flea)

Professor
Ratticus

2

LOOK OUT FOR THESE
CHARACTERS—THEY
ARE YOUR GUIDES
THROUGH THE DARK
CORRIDORS OF THE
GERM LAB

Lab assistant Tik-Tik
(a tsetse fly)

Lab assistant Mozzy
(a mosquito)

DATES IN THE BOOK

A.D.: this means "anno Domini" and refers to the period of measured time that begins with A.D. 1 (also known as the "common era").

B.C.: this means "before Christ" and refers to any dates before A.D. 1. For example, 100 BC means "100 years before A.D. 1."before the Common Era'.

3

IN THE GERM LAB

Welcome to the Germ Lab, home of horrible diseases. But be careful! Catching one could make you ill.

Pass the infection to others and you might start an epidemic in which thousands perish . . . But wait! Don't you know there are ways to stop deadly diseases these days?

UNKNOWN GERMS

EBOLA VIRUS

TUBERCULOSIS

History's epidemic villains

Germs do not always spread disease on their own. Some of them get help. Black rats, for example, spread bubonic plague (see pages 14 to 17). And, in fact, it is the fleas on the rats' backs that actually pass on this harmful bacteria. Rats spread more than 40 human diseases, but they

are not the only animal villains out there. Mosquitoes, snails, birds, and even dogs and cats also carry illnesses. See how many carriers of disease you can spot as you tour the GERM LAB.

Professor Ratticus

PLAGUE

KNOW YOUR GERMS

Three kinds of germs spread illness.
Protists are tiny living creatures.
Even tinier, bacteria are the smallest known living things.
Viruses are even smaller, but they are not alive.
They trick our bodies into copying them
until there is enough virus to be dangerous.

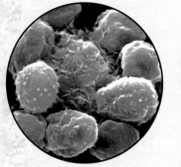

Red blood cells infected
with the *Plasmodium*
protist, which causes
malaria

Yersinia pestis bacterium
(causes bubonic plague)

Variola virus
(causes smallpox)

NOW THAT'S SMALL!

Germs are tiny! In the
width of just one human
hair you could fit 200
Plasmodium protists or
500 bubonic plague bacteria
or 3,300 *Variola* viruses.

Some germs do useful
things, such as turning
dead plants into soil.

RABIES

GERMS

FLU
VIRUS

UNDER THE MICROSCOPE

Germs are invisible to the naked eye. In fact, it was only the invention of the microscope in the 1600s that allowed scientists to see the pesky critters at all. Microscopes use lenses to magnify germs so that the experts in the lab can identify them.

BRING 'EM CLOSER!

A laboratory microscope uses two lenses to make things look much larger than they really are. An "objective" lens near the bottom enlarges whatever is right underneath it. Then, an "eyepiece" lens at the top of the microscope magnifies the image again.

BIGGER BACTERIA

You can see bacteria using a microscope that magnifies 100 times. They breed fast to form vast groups called colonies. Bacteria are found everywhere but only a few spread disease.

THE FIRST MICROSCOPE

The first person to see germs was a Dutch scientist named Antoni van Leeuwenhoek (left). He used a thumb-size microscope with tiny glass beads for lenses. He studied protists and bacteria in the late 1600s but never guessed they caused disease.

A CLOSER LOOK AT PROTISTS

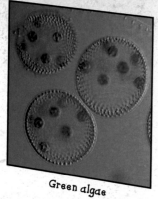

Green algae

A little bigger than bacteria, protists are easy to see with a microscope. They like wet places. Some, such as algae (left), feed on light as plants do. Others are more like animals and wiggle around searching for food.

MAGNIFYING VIRUSES

Viruses are so small that it takes a powerful electron microscope to see them. They invade body cells—the "building blocks" of all living things. Once inside, a virus forces the cell to make more and more identical viruses. This damages the cell, causing disease.

An electron micropscope image of influenze virus particles

Ordinary microscopes use light to form enlarged pictures. But viruses are smaller than light beams, so they look fuzzy. Instead, scientists point a beam of electrons—tiny particles—at viruses. An electron microscope (right) can magnify up to two million times.

DISEASE: HOW IT SPREADS

The Germ Lab is under attack! Beware infection! It's bad news and can mean discomfort, pain, or even death. Most harmful germs cause obvious signs of disease, called symptoms. They leave their victims just well enough to infect others. Each infected person multiplies the number of germs and the disease spreads with ease.

THE SPY GERM

Some germs hide in a victim's body without causing any symptoms. The infected person then spreads the disease to others without knowing it. For example, leprosy sufferers can spread the disease on their breath for up to 20 years before showing any signs of illness themselves (see page 18).

PASSING IT ON

For germs that cause illness, infection means success. That's why they have found so many clever ways to get inside our bodies. Here are the most common:

 BY MOUTH: infections enter our guts on food, in drinks, or from dirty hands.

IN BLOOD: diseases spread though open wounds or dirty syringes.

 FROM ANIMALS: living things such as lice, fleas, or flies can pass on infections.

FROM OBJECTS: germs linger on things we handle, such as doorknobs, coins, or dollar bills.

FROM DROPLETS: sick people infect others by coughing, sneezing, or breathing.

THROUGH SEX: some diseases cause infection through sexual contact.

THE WARRIOR GERM

Some infections cause dramatic symptoms that spread a disease rapidly. Cholera bacteria (see page 22) work like this. Anyone swallowing them soon suffers from terrible vomiting and diarrhea. Gallons of liquid spill from their guts, carrying millions of cholera bacteria. If the diarrhea pollutes drinking water, the disease spreads in no time.

THE WAR ON GERMS

A pandemic is an outbreak of disease that makes people sick on several continents or even worldwide. The worst pandemics can kill millions of people.

A PANDEMIC NEVER WIPES OUT THE WORLD

Here's why:

- We all have a natural way of fighting off dangerous diseases. It is called the immune response (see page 32).

- The most successful germs kill only a few of the people they infect. If viruses or bacteria killed everyone they infected, there would be no one left to pass on the disease.

- Through scientific research, we have developed ways to stop diseases from spreading.

NORTH
AMERICA

Smallpox
1781

ATLANTIC
OCEAN

HIV
early 1980s
onward

Smallpox
1530

SOUTH
AMERICA

EGYPT

INDIA

CANADA

10

MODERN PANDEMIC

In March 2020 a new global pandemic was declared as the infectious disease coronavirus (COVID-19) quickly spread around the world.

(see pages 14–17)

(see page 30)

FOUR GLOBAL PANDEMICS

Diseases have crossed continents with soldiers, travelers, traders, and explorers.

BLACK DEATH 1347: the bubonic plague (see pages 14–17) swept through Asia and Europe in the 1300s.

SMALLPOX 1530 and 1781: the smallpox virus (see page 30) traveled to America with European explorers and settlers.

HONG KONG FLU 1968–69: soldiers returning from war in Vietnam carried this Asian flu pandemic to the United States.

HIV 1980s onwards: originally a disease of chimpanzees, what we now call HIV spread through Africa in the 1930s and 1950s. By the 1980s, it had become a global pandemic.

Disease of the Day: CHOLERA

EUROPE

HIV early 1980s onward

ASIA

Black Death (bubonic plague) 1347

AFRICA

HIV origin? (date unknown)

PACIFIC OCEAN

Hong Kong Flu 1968–1969

PACIFIC OCEAN

CORPSE CATAPULT

In 1347, Asian warriors attacking the town of Caffa, Ukraine, used a trebuchet to hurl diseased bodies over the town walls in order to infect those inside. This helped spread the bubonic plague to Europe.

A medieval trebuchet, or catapult

☞ TYPHUS

Infection: bacteria, spread by the bite of a louse.

Typhus spreads quickly in crowded, dirty places. An epidemic in the 30 Years' War (1618–1648) killed up to one-third of all Germans. Typhus is now cured with antibiotics.

☞ YELLOW FEVER

Infection: a virus, spread by a mosquito bite.

Symptoms include yellowing of the skin and bleeding from the eyes, nose, and mouth. A vaccine protects against it, but there is no cure. An 1878 epidemic in the United States killed 20,000 people.

☞ TYPHOID

Infection: bacteria, spread by sewage in food or water.

Typhoid affects 17 million people annually, killing some 600,000. Symptoms include fever and diarrhea. Clean water and soap can help stop its spread, and it can be cured using antibiotics.

THE ROGUES' GALLERY

Before exploring the Germ Lab to learn more about the worst diseases, take a look at this Rogues' Gallery of germs—proof that disease comes in many disguises.

DENGUE

Infection: a virus, spread by mosquito bites.
This disease threatens two-fifths of the world's people. Sufferers have painful joints and are treated using painkillers and sweet drinks. There is no prevention or cure.

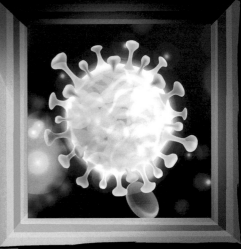

POLIO

Infection: a virus, spread by sewage in food or water.
Polio infects young children and withers their muscles. In 1952, 3,500 Americans died of polio. Vaccination now protects children from the disease.

CORONAVIRUS (COVID-19)

Infection: a virus, spread by droplets from the mouth or nose from an infected person.
Discovered in Wuhan, China, in December 2019, this infectious disease was classed as a pandemic as it spread around the world. Symptoms include fever, tiredness, and a dry cough. Scientists developed the first COVID-19 vaccines in 2020.

☞ HIV

Infection: a virus (right), spread by sexual contact or through infected blood.
Short for human immunodeficiency virus, HIV stops a patient's body from fighting off deadly infections. With the right care, people can live for many years with HIV, but it still kills about two million people every year.

To protect against infection, doctors wore beaked masks and prodded sufferers with sticks. The "cures" they offered were useless.

1. Healthy rat

2. Infected flea bites rat

3. Rat dies

4. Fleas flee to human

5. Flea bites human

6. Rest in peace

SPREADING THE PLAGUE

Fleas living on rats spread this disease. They caught it from infected rats and spread it by biting healthy rats. When a rat died of the disease, its fleas hopped onto people, passing it to them, too.

BLACK DEATH

Rats riddled the streets in 14th-century towns, gobbling food and leaving trails of filth. In 1347, they also spread the bubonic plague. Dubbed the "Black Death" after the horrible swellings on victims' bodies, this deadly disease killed more than one-third of all Europeans.

HOW TO SPOT IT . . .

Signs appeared within two to ten days of a flea bite. Sufferers developed a sudden high fever. Some got terrible headaches and backaches. Others coughed and vomited blood. If smooth swellings, called buboes, appeared in the neck, armpits, or groin, a painful death was just days away.

. . . AND HOW TO STOP IT

Governments tried to stop the plague. In 1397, in the Croatian city of Dubrovnik, the council made all arriving visitors stay on a nearby island. Only those still healthy after 30 days (later 40 days) were let into the city. This time of closely watched separation was called quarantine, after the Italian quaranta giorni ("40 days").

THE SEARCH FOR A CURE

Wealthy sufferers swallowed drinks made mostly from plants and trees. If these did not work, a doctor opened the patient's veins to let the blood run out. The poor could only pray they would escape death. Priests urged them to avoid luxury, hot baths, fruit, and naughty behavior. None of these measures stopped people from dying.

THE PLAGUE SPREADS!

The Black Death crossed continents, hitching a ride with infected rats, fleas, and people. It reached southeast Europe in 1347. By autumn of 1348, it was killing people in Britain. Whenever it reached a new town, citizens fled—many not knowing they were infected. They carried the plague to the next town . . . and the next . . .

STARVATION followed the plague, because the disease killed workers who grew food plants and stopped the trade in grain.

FLEEING by road or by ship was a luxury only the rich could afford. Travel was expensive, and poor people could not flee.

HOW MANY GRAVES?

Experts think the 14th-century outbreak of Black Death killed up to 50 million people in Europe and Asia.

THE SPREAD OF THE BUBONIC PLAGUE (BLACK DEATH)

Areas affected by 1347

Areas affected by 1348

Areas affected by 1349

AREAS AFFECTED BY 1350–1352, OR NOT AT ALL

NORTH SEA

ATLANTIC OCEAN

MEDITERRANEAN SEA

1350

1349

1349

1348

London

1349 Cologne

1348 Paris

1349 Mainz

Strasbourg

1349

1348–49

Lyon

Bordeaux

1348

1348

Genoa

Toulouse

Marseilles

Aix

1347

1349

1348

1347

Toledo

Barcelona

1348

1348

1348

1348

Valencia

1348

1347

PENITENTS whipped themselves. They believed the disease was God's punishment for human wickedness and thought their suffering would save lives.

BLAME for the Black Death fell on Jews, lepers, and Romani (Gypsy) people—all victims of ancient prejudice.

A CURE AT LAST!

Epidemics tailed off after the 1600s, though nobody knows why. Antibiotic drugs (see page 41) finally provided a cure. Today, for every 20 people infected and treated, only one dies.

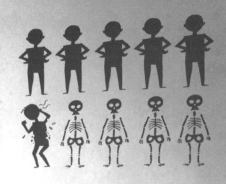

LUCKY TO BE ALIVE

The Black Death killed between one-third and one-half of all Europeans. City dwellers around the Mediterranean Sea were most likely to die, while more people survived in the countryside areas of northern Europe.

1350
BALTIC SEA
Novgorod
1352
Copenhagen
1350
Moscow
1352
Lübeck
1350
1350
1351
Venice
1348
1347
Caffa
BLACK SEA
1347
Rome
1348
Constantinople (now Istanbul)
Naples
1347
1348
Athens
1348
Messina
1347

Leprosy began in eastern Africa, and migration carried it into Europe and Asia. Later, lepers were among the West African people captured by European merchants and transported to the Caribbean islands and South America to work as slaves.

Medieval priests used Bible stories to convince people that leprosy was God's punishment for evil.

NORTH AMERICA

EUROPE

ASIA

Caribbean Sea

ATLANTIC OCEAN

West Africa

SOUTH AMERICA

Brazil

"UNCLEAN, UNCLEAN!"

A hooded beggar hobbles down a medieval street. He rings a bell and croaks "Unclean" to warn that he is coming. Children stare at his damaged body. Adults leave food for him but shrink from his touch. They don't want to catch his disease: leprosy!

AN ANCIENT DISEASE

The oldest physical evidence of this disease is from Jerusalem, in the Middle East. In 2009, archaeologists digging in the Hinnom Valley found leprosy bacteria in the body of a man buried in a cave there some 2,000 years ago.

The leper's tomb found near Jerusalem was well preserved because the entrance was sealed.

THE DREADED LEPER

Modern drugs cure leprosy, which is a danger to one in every 20 people. But 800 years ago, the disease was a frightening mystery. Lepers had to wear special marks, such as yellow crosses, and were locked up in colonies, away from other people.

Lepers shook a warning bell or wooden clapper.

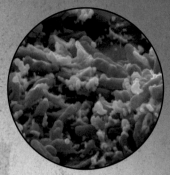

Tuberculosis bacteria

DISEASE OR DEFENSE?

Fewer leprosy epidemics occurred in Europe after 1300, possibly because people started living in cities. Another disease, tuberculosis (see page 42), spread quickly in the crowded and dirty streets, and we now know that catching tuberculosis protects against leprosy.

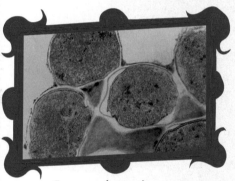

Leprosy bacteria

The damaged hand of a leprosy sufferer

Leprosy may be caught by breathing infected droplets in the air. It can be 20 years before a victim develops visible symptoms—patches of thick, numb skin that turn into crusty swellings.

TRUE OR FALSE?

Leprosy makes body parts fall off? FALSE! But because they feel numb, sufferers are more likely to injure themselves and lose limbs that way.

A DEADLY DEBATE

Two hundred years ago, doctors argued about the causes of disease. Without scientific explanations of how diseases spread, doctors could do little to stop them. Common ideas on how people got sick were ancient—and mostly wrong . . .

THE HUMORS

Since around 400 B.C., Doctors had taken the "theory of humors" seriously. Humors (they believed) were four liquids that filled human bodies: blood, phlegm (snot), yellow bile, and black bile. For good health, the four humors had to be in balance. If they were not, sickness was the result. This theory was wrong.

MIASMA

Doctors had known since AD 1 that people became sick near swamps, sewers, and piles of filth. They thought harmful gases called "miasmas" spread from these places. They were wrong.

BLOOD: air, spring

PHLEGM: water, winter

YELLOW BILE: fire, summer

BLACK BILE: earth, autumn

Each of the humors was linked to a season and to one of the elements— the four kinds of matter from which ancient people believed everything was made.

SIN

Religious leaders saw illness as God's punishment for wrong-doing, but epidemics made this hard to accept. Countless good and deeply religious people died, while the wicked and godless often survived.

CONTAGION

In the 1300s, Arab scholars suggested that sickness began when "minute bodies" invaded a healthy person. A century later, Italian physician Fracastorius agreed. He blamed "disease seeds" for causing infection and thought they could pass between people on infected objects, such as clothes. His ideas were ridiculed.

21

THE MEDICAL DETECTIVE

Most "experts" thought a miasma (see page 20) caused cholera. But doctor John Snow believed polluted water was to blame. He talked to people living in Soho, a London neighborhood badly hit by the epidemic. Slum dwellers told him how many people had died and where they had lived. Snow plotted the deaths on a map (far right), and his map proved that water was indeed the cause.

Many Soho families shared one lavatory, often just a hole in the ground with a seat above it.

A HAND PUMP drew water from a well on Broad Street. Snow removed the pump handle, forcing people to drink from other wells. Almost immediately, the Soho epidemic ended. Snow's hunch had been right. Cholera spread when a victim used a lavatory and sewage from it seeped into a underground well.

THE UNWELL WELL

Bad smells had long been part of London life, but in 1854 the stink was worse than usual. An epidemic of the world's most deadly stomach upset gripped the city: cholera. The disease was killing thousands, but what was its cause?

John Snow (1813–1858) was a respected physician, but other doctors laughed at his ideas about the spread of cholera.

SOHO, LONDON, 1854

Broad Street

SNOW'S MAP

Marking a bar where each cholera victim died showed that most used a well on Broad Street. Snow guessed the water was polluted.

SUDDEN FEVER

Cholera symptoms include violent, watery diarrhea and a bad stomachache. Loss of fluid dries out victims' bodies, shrinking them and turning their skin blue—as shown in this medical book illustration from 1833.

NEW SEWERS

Others eventually accepted Snow's ideas. In 1859, construction began on a system of sewers for London—huge pipes that collected human waste from lavatories and carried it safely away. The city never suffered from a cholera epidemic again.

This drawing, from the time of the epidemic, shows the figure of Death working the Broad Street pump.

This photograph shows the construction of the London sewerage system in 1859.

BUG BREAKTHROUGH

It was in the 1800s that three great scientists—Louis Pasteur, Robert Koch, and Ferdinand Cohn—proved that germs spread disease. They also found ways to prevent them from spreading.

Louis Pasteur (1822–1895) working in his laboratory

In his laboratory at the University of Lille, France, biologist Louis Pasteur tried to find out why wine and beer sometimes went bad. He showed that drinks soured when microbes (germs) from the air drifted into them. By gently heating the beer and wine, Pasteur killed off the microbes and preserved the drinks for longer. The same process preserved cow's milk, too. The germ-killing heat treatment was named "pasteurization." Pasteur also observed broth (meat soup) going bad. To prove

Germ Theory

that microbes drifting in the air turned the soup bad, he first heated two samples to kill off the microbes. He then left one sample open to the air. Microbes settled on it, and mold grew. He placed the other sample in a flask with a curved neck. The U-shaped bend trapped the microbes, and no mold grew on the broth inside.

SAFER MILK

Once we knew people could get tuberculosis from contaminated milk, pasteurization equipment was installed in farms and factories (above). All store-bought milk is pasteurized today.

MICROBE HUNTERS

Two German scientists also studied microbes. Ferdinand Cohn named the different types of bacteria, and Robert Koch identified the bacteria that caused anthrax, tuberculosis, and cholera infections. Tuberculosis was a major killer at the time, and Koch's work led to a vaccine (see page 43) to protect against it.

Robert Koch
(1843–1910)

Ferdinand Cohn
(1828–1898)

Koch, Cohn, and Pasteur launched the science of microbiology: the study of living things too small to see with the naked eye.

DEATH IN THE AIR

In hot, wet countries, mosquitoes can spread a dangerous disease called malaria. Sufferers have a fever that makes them hot and sweaty one minute, then freezing cold the next. The fever returns every two days. Without treatment, malaria causes damage to the blood that can lead to death.

1. Mosquito is infected

5. New mosquito takes infected red blood cells from the victim

LIFE OF A KILLER

The protist *Plasmodium* causes malaria. When a mosquito feeds on a sufferer, it sucks up *Plasmodium* with the blood. When the insect bites again, it injects the protist into the victim's blood. In the human body, *Plasmodium* multiplies in the liver and blood. Damaged blood cells stick together, causing deadly blockages in arteries (blood pipes).

2. Parasites spread in mosquito's gut

4. Parasites move to the human liver

3. Infection injected into a human

SWAMPS AND MARSHES

People once called malaria "swamp fever" because there were more sufferers near marshland than anywhere else. They thought bad vapors rising from the swamps caused the disease.

26

EARLY REMEDIES

In 17th-century Peru, malaria sufferers chewed the bark of the cinchona shrub. The healing chemical in the bark is called quinine. Chinese healers used to treat malaria with an herb called sweet wormwood— an extract from this is the source of a modern malaria drug called artemisinin.

MODERN REMEDIES

Malaria is a big problem in Africa, South Asia, and South America, but preventing it is simple. Mosquitoes feed at night, so covering beds in insecticide-soaked nets stops them from biting. Sadly, the people most at risk are too poor to buy the nets, and a million die each year. Most are young children.

Spraying an insecticide

Mosquito nets over beds

In ancient times, migrating people spread malaria to the Middle East and Asia.

Malaria spread through Europe, c. A.D. 500–1500.

EUROPE

ASIA

Greece, c. 300 B.C.

China, c. 2700 B.C.

NORTH AMERICA

Italy, c. 200 B.C.

Northern India, c.1000 B.C.

Atlantic Ocean

Egypt, c. 1500 B.C.

AFRICA

More than 30 million years ago, malaria parasites infected apes and ancient humans.

SOUTH AMERICA

European explorers carried malaria to North and South America starting c. A.D. 1500.

WORLDWIDE EXPANSION

Malaria leaves no marks on skeletons, so scientists are unable to trace its spread by studying old human remains. However, throughout history, writers have described malaria's symptoms, and we can follow its deadly path using their stories (see above).

THE RESISTANCE

In 2009, malaria sufferers in Thailand and Cambodia failed to respond to treatment. The *Plasmodium* protists in their blood had developed a resistance to the usual drugs. New drugs are now in use, and health officials are working hard to wipe out this new, more dangerous form of the disease.

CHILDHOOD DISEASES

There was no escaping death's bony hand in the slums of 19th-century cities. As many as one in three children died before their first birthday. Until there was better housing—and routine vaccination—cities remained deadly places.

CROWDED CITIES

The poor often lived in cramped homes shared by other families. In New York City, tall buildings called "tenements" were split into dozens of tiny rooms, most without windows, running water, or toilets. Disease raced through them in summer: more than 100 children died each day in July 1876.

A DISEASE OF DEADLY SPOTS

Measles is passed on in the air that sufferers breathe out, and in mucus from their nose and mouth. It spreads very easily and once killed one-fourth of all the slum children who caught it. Those who survived became immune (they could not catch it again). As immunity levels rose, measles outbreaks ended naturally, only to return when immunity levels fell.

Child-size coffins were a common sight in the 1800s.

Portrait of emperor
Gordian I on a coin

GROWING OLD

Anyone who survived childhood
stood a good chance of living a long
life. In ancient Rome, three out of
every ten people died as babies, and
yet a ten-year-old could expect to
live to be 50. The Roman emperor
Gordian, for example, was 79 when
he died, in A.D. 238.

A whole gang of infections killed off children
around this time. Whooping cough was the biggest
killer of under-fives. Many also died of diphtheria,
German measles, mumps and scarlet fever.

GETTING VACCINATED

In the 20th century, vaccination by injection (see page 33)
made children immune to many germs. By 1920, scientists
had developed "shots" for diphtheria and whooping cough.
Those for measles, mumps, and German measles followed
in the 1960s. In some countries, shots are required by law
before children start school.

CURING THE POX

In the stuffy darkness of an Egyptian tomb, archaeologists jump back in alarm as they prize open a stone coffin. Blisters cover the face of the long-dead pharaoh within: smallpox! This deadly disease claimed millions of lives around the world—until vaccination wiped it out for good in the 1980s.

The 12th-century B.C. pharaoh Rameses V died of smallpox.

Blisters are so close together that some victims have blisters on their blisters!

Survivors of the disease were left scarred for life.

THE BIRTH OF A DISEASE

Scientists think smallpox began when wandering people started farming and living in larger groups some 12,000 years ago. It probably started as an illness of farm animals in Africa or Asia. It may have infected humans when we began sheltering farm animals in our homes.

SMALLPOX EPIDEMICS

People infected with smallpox remained healthy for almost two weeks—enough time to spread the virus. China saw epidemics in the 300s. The disease spread to Japan in the 730s. A Persian doctor named Rhazes wrote about the disease in the 900s, when it was common in Europe, Asia, and Africa. Epidemics in Europe were killing 400,000 people annually 800 years later.

USELESS REMEDIES

There were many "cures" for smallpox, none of which worked. The Japanese bathed in a soup of rice wine, beans, and salt. Brazilians rubbed horse dung on the blisters. Indians avoided fried and spicy food. European doctors drained their patients' blood. People even believed that wearing the color red would cure the disease.

Bathing in a soothing mineral bath was thought to ease the suffering.

EXPORTING A KILLER

When Europeans traveled to America in the 1500s, they took smallpox with them. The Native Americans had no resistance to the virus, and millions died. In Mexico alone, it killed about one-third of the population in just six months.

THE REAL CURE

People in Africa and the Middle East developed a preventative treatment for smallpox: nonsufferers broke their own skin and rubbed in pus drawn from a blister on the skin of a sufferer. This protection saved the lives of five out of every six children who later caught the disease. African slave Onesimus introduced the method, called inoculation, to Americans around 1713. English noblewoman Mary Wortley Montagu learned it in Turkey four years later.

A bronze statuette of Onesimus

Lady Mary Wortley Montagu

31

FIGHTING BACK

Nasty germs would have wiped us all out long ago if it hadn't been for our immune system. This natural defence guards against infections and helps us recover from them. It has a memory, which protects us from suffering the same disease twice. Immunization gives us similar protection—without us having to catch an infection in the first place!

WHITE BLOOD CELLS

IMMUNE SYSTEM: ARCHIVE DEPT.

TOXINS

VIRAL INFECTIONS

PLAGUE BACTERIA

NATURAL IMMUNITY

Most of the immune system is hidden in our blood. White blood cells surround germs and kill them. When we catch a disease for the first time, the white blood cells produce chemicals called antibodies. These stay in the blood, ready to take action should the same type of germ attack again.

UNKNOWN PATHOGENS

This virus cell (purple) is surrounded by Y-shaped antibody molecules.

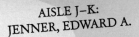

A DARING DOCTOR

In 1773, an English doctor named Edward Jenner (below) treated a milkmaid for cowpox—a mild disease caught from cows. She boasted that this infection protected her from smallpox. During a smallpox epidemic in 1788, Jenner noticed that any patient who had suffered cowpox escaped smallpox. Daringly, he infected his gardener's son with cowpox, and then later with smallpox. The boy recovered from cowpox, and never caught smallpox. This was the start of immunization.

JENNER,
EDWARD A.
(1749–1823)

IMMUNIZATION

Jenner developed the first "vaccine." Vaccines trigger the immune system to make antibodies that fight just one kind of germ. Today many different vaccines exist. Global use of the smallpox vaccine completely killed off the disease by 1980.

PROTECTING EVERYONE

New vaccines undergo painstaking trials before being used on people. They are sometimes the only protection against incurable diseases. They work best when doctors give them to everyone at risk of infection. When vaccination first began in the 1700s, people doubted it. Cartoons such as this (right) spread fear.

PARASITIC
WORMS

A WARTIME KILLER

Millions died during World War I (1914–1918), but not all were killed by bullets and bombs. No—by far the biggest killer was influenza, a virus that is still so common we forget how dangerous it can be. It spreads quickly and changes to avoid the safeguards we invent to protect against it.

THE FLU VIRUS

Influenza is not just a bad cold. The virus (left) gives you a fever, sore throat, headache, and a cough, and makes you weak and achy. Coughs and sneezes spread the virus in tiny, moist droplets. The virus can change and adapt, so catching one strain, or variety, of the flu may not make you immune to another.

A KILLER STALKS . . .

Every year, the flu kills between 250,000 and 500,000 people worldwide. From time to time, a new and more deadly strain causes a pandemic. The first global outbreak of the flu occurred in 1889. The worst was in 1918, when half the world's population became infected and at least 40 million people died.

A Spanish flu ward, 1918

DIFFERENT KINDS OF FLU

Flu viruses can jump from humans to some birds and animals, and back again, especially if the two species live close together. When the virus makes such a leap, it changes. Scientists give each type of flu a number to identify it. For example, bird flu is H5N1.

WHO IS IN DANGER?

Some people are more at risk of dying in a flu pandemic. They include:

 SUFFERERS of conditions such as asthma, or those with a weak immune system.

 OLDER PEOPLE may have a weaker immunity to influenza.

 PREGNANT WOMEN are often infected much more easily.

STOPPING THE VIRUS

Scientists created the first flu vaccine in the 1940s, but the flu changes quickly, and vaccines work for only a couple of years. When each new strain emerges, medical researchers quickly identify it and develop a new vaccine. Drug companies race to produce enough doses to protect the vulnerable before they become infected.

BLIGHT AND FAMINE

Would you be scared of a disease that attacks only a plant? What if the plant's leaves, roots, or fruits were all you had to eat? We rely on plants for all of our meals: we wouldn't have meat without plants to feed farm animals. So when crops (food plants) fail, hunger and famine can soon follow.

Starving families plead for food (above).

POTATO FAMINE

A million Irish people died during the Great Hunger of the mid-1800s. The cause? Potato blight, a mold that destroyed whole fields of potatoes in days. People were weakened by starvation, leaving them more likely to catch diseases such as typhus.

FINDING SOLUTIONS

People in Africa eat more cassava roots than any other food. So when disease strikes the plant, millions face starvation. Scientists worked for ten years to improve this vital crop (below). By breeding the most popular cassava with more unusual varieties, they produced a range of new, more resistant plants.

Salmonella
bacterium

E. coli
bacteria

THE TROUBLE WITH GRUB

In developed countries, food often comes from factories or farms miles away from the supermarkets that sell it. Bad handling or storage of the food can introduce harmful bacteria. For example, deadly salmonella bacteria can lurk in unclean or badly prepared food. Poorly washed vegetables might harbor harmful E. coli bacteria.

CROP DESTROYERS

In modern times, a few high-tech crops promising big harvests have pushed aside a wider range of traditional varieties. If all farmers plant these new crops, they risk entire harvests being destroyed by disease, with little or no backup.

A 'black stem rust' infection on wheat

FUNGUS AND FEVER

A frightened young woman lies twitching and twisting on the floor. She sees visions and feels prickling and bites on her arms. Three hundred years ago, she would have been taken for a witch! Today, we would know that she had eaten bread containing a nasty fungus called ergot.

ERGOT'S ALARMING SIGNS

The disease ergotism takes two forms. One targets the brain and nerves. The other strangles the arteries that channel blood to our limbs.

SHAKING AND TWITCHING

As ergot damages nerves, sufferers' bodies twitch and bend into unnatural shapes. They feel numbness and "pins and needles" on their skin.

SEEING VISIONS

Ergot contains a chemical that causes hallucinations. Sufferers may see or hear things that exist only in their minds.

LOSING LIMBS

When ergotism damages the arteries, fingers and toes blister, redden, and go numb. It cuts off the flow of blood to the feet and hands and their flesh dies.

INFECTED GRAIN

Ergot fungus grows on rye grain in damp weather. Anxious farmers might be tempted to overlook the blackened tips that are a sure sign of attack. In large quantities the fungus stains flour red when the grain is ground. But rye flour is dark in color so ergot often goes unnoticed. A tiny amount of fungus can cause an epidemic.

Ergot fungus growing on ears of rye

AMERICAN WITCHES?

At the end of the 1600s, young girls in the village of Salem, Massachusetts, began screaming, having seizures, and complaining of being pricked with pins. They were put on trial as witches and executed. The cause of the outbreak remains unknown, but it is possible they had eaten rye bread containing ergot.

A child writhes on the floor at the Salem witch trials.

BREAD SPREADS DEATH

Ergotism hit northern Europe the worst, as rye was the only grain that would grow there. Historians estimate that two out of every five sufferers died. Here are some of the most serious epidemics:

 FRANCE, A.D. 922: an epidemic killed 40,000 people.

 FRANCE, 1128: 14,000 people died in an outbreak in the capital, Paris.

 GERMANY, 1374: Ergotism may have caused a "dancing fever" that swept through Aix-La-Chapelle (Aachen).

 RUSSIA, 1722: 20,000 died, including thousands of soldiers, forcing the Russian emperor to call off a war.

 FINLAND, 1862–1863: a famine forced people to eat whatever they could find—1,400 caught ergotism.

MODERN DANGERS

Everyone in the Germ Lab remains on red alert. Why? After two hundred years of medical research, deadly epidemics continue to threaten our health. The dangers are even increasing. Modern threats come from food, warfare, and the misuse of drugs. The biggest hazard of all? Vacations overseas!

GERMS ON BOARD

Scientists have long known that bugs hitch rides on planes, but it was only in 2003 that they realized how serious this could be. The first case of severe acute respiratory syndrome (SARS) appeared in China at the end of February 2003. By mid-April, it ha[s] spread to 24 countries. Travel restrictions cannot stop diseases spreading—they or delay them by a couple of weeks or so.

WE CAN'T KEEP EATING LIKE THIS!

Animals are often farmed close together, and in large numbers, before being processed for food. Disease can spread rapidly, infecting whole countries when once they would have poisoned only a village. In the 1980s, British people ate meat from half a million cattle suffering from BSE ("mad cow" disease) before scientists realized the danger to the public. Raising animals closer to where they are eaten, on smaller farms, and in better conditions could end such hazards.

A large number of cattle feed together in an intensive "feed lot"

LOCKDOWN!

As coronavirus (COVID-19) spread around the world, infecting millions of people and causing the death of thousands, many governments put strict measures in place.

A person catches COVID-19 from someone already with the virus. Small droplets produced by a contagious person coughing or sneezing can be breathed in or land on touchable surfaces, leading others to possibly become infected. The advice worldwide is to cough and sneeze into a tissue, dispose of the tissue and to wash hands regularly and thoroughly. From the start of 2020, nation by nation imposed a lockdown on its citizens. Schools, sports centers, places of worship, and many other public buildings were closed and everyone advised to stay indoors. By implementing such stringent measures, the spread rate of the virus slowed down. National vaccination programs also helped to fight the virus and save lives.

A medical worker disinfecting a Chinese passenger plane in 2003.

GO THE FULL COURSE!

Antibiotics kill bacteria if the dose is strong enough and the patient takes all the pills. However, some patients share pills, or stop taking them when they start to feel better. Then the bacteria don't die. Even worse, they find ways to protect themselves against the antibiotics. Limiting the use of antibiotics can help prevent this.

X-RAY RESCUE

To its 19th-century victims, "consumption" was a slow but determined killer. Named for its ability to eat up (or 'consume') sufferers, the disease was incurable. Today, doctors call the disease tuberculosis (TB). They can spot it in a chest X-ray and prescribe antibiotics to cure it.

X-ray image of the lungs, showing TB's wispy shadows (top left)

COUGH OF DEATH

The telltale sign of TB is coughing. TB bacteria destroy the lungs, and sufferers spit out blood. Most also have a high body temperature and pale skin, and suffer weight loss because they have no appetite. Before there was a cure, wealthy sufferers stayed in special clinics far from their city homes. They rested in outdoor beds, soaking up sunshine and breathing clean, fresh air.

THE "TB" SUFFERER

Night sweats

Rosy cheeks

Hacking cough

Weight loss

Pale skin

Uncontrollable shivering

BONE MARROW AND TB
Advanced TB kills blood-making marrow inside a sufferer's bones. Archaeologists can spot marks left 3,000 years ago.

LOOKING AT THE LUNGS

In 1895, German scientist Wilhelm Röntgen discovered invisible beams that passed through solid objects. Named X-rays, they allowed doctors to look inside the body without cutting it open. Within two years, doctors had begun using them to make pictures of patients' lungs. Tuberculosis showed up as cloudy shadows, offering a quick way to spot the disease.

CELEBRITY SUFFERERS

Tuberculosis killed so many famous people in the 1700s and 1800s that it became almost a fashionable way to die. The Romantic painters and writers liked to think it affected creative types more than others, but this was not true. In fact, TB was most likely to kill the poor, who lived in crowded places or in dirty, airless homes where TB bacteria can thrive. Hunger meant that poorer people could not fight off the disease as easily.

The mummy of Egyptian woman Irtyersenu, who died of TB about 2,600 years ago.

Napoleon II (1811-1832)—French emperor for 15 days at the age of four—died of TB when he was only 21 years old.

Lead aprons protect against absorbing too many X-rays.

Eleanor Roosevelt (1884-1962) was the very popular wife of President Franklin D. Roosevelt. TB played a part in her death.

The telltale scar of the BCG shot

RETURN OF THE KILLER

By the mid-20th century, antibiotic drugs could cure TB. But the disease soon developed antibiotic resistance (see page 41). In 2006, patients in South Africa began to die from a form of TB that no drug could cure. Disease-control agencies now fear that the threat of TB may, in the future, be as great as it was 100 years ago.

A SHOT FOR TB

Preventing TB is easier than curing it, and a vaccine called the BCG does just that. Most children who get the shot cannot catch some forms of TB. Protection is not always reliable, though, and wears off after 20 years or so.

THE FUTURE

The future could prove challenging. New diseases are appearing all the time, and old ones that we thought were under control are returning to threaten our health. Viruses and bacteria mutate (change), so it is vital that people get the right information and take the correct treatments for them.

NEW WAYS TO GET VERY SICK

The crack team at the Germ Lab is tracking four nasty diseases: the Ebola and Nipah viruses, bird flu, and swine flu. All four come from animals. Ebola and Nipah have alarming symptoms and are often fatal. The two flu viruses are major pandemic threats.

KEY

EBOLA VIRUS: began in 1976, in Zaire, killing nine out of every ten people infected.

NIPAH VIRUS: first spread from fruit bats to humans in Malaysia, in 1999.

BIRD FLU: spread from chickens to humans in 2004, in Southeast Asia.

SWINE FLU: jumped from pigs to humans in 2009.

NORTH AMERICA

SOUTH AMERICA

EUROPE

AFRICA

Zaire (now Democratic Republic of Congo)

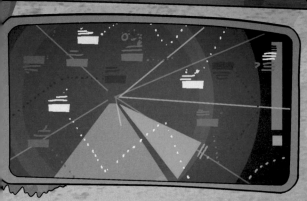

HUNTING A VIRUS

Most new diseases come from farm animals, apes, and monkeys. One way to predict pandemics is to check the health of people who hunt or care for these animals, since they are the first to get sick when disease spreads. Dr. Nathan Wolfe of Global Virus Forecasting does just this, mostly in tropical Africa and Southeast Asia.

"Virus-hunter"
Dr. Nathan Wolfe

BEATING DISEASE

Developing treatments for infections— and vaccines to prevent them—is costly, and it is not always necessary. The best protection against cholera is clean water and soap, while a $2 bed net can stop a child from catching malaria. Still, governments need money to buy these things, networks to distribute them, and people who understand how to use them.

THINKING GLOBALLY

To support the world's governments, international organizations take the lead in controlling pandemics. For 70 years, the World Health Organization (WHO) has managed worldwide disease control. WHO drew up the International Health Regulations that aim to stop epidemics from crossing continents. Many other organizations and charities work alongside it.

The emblem of the
World Health Organization

ASIA

Malaysia

AUSTRALIA

GERM TERMS

antibiotic
A medical drug that stops infections caused by bacteria.

antibody
A protein the body produces in response to, and to protect against, a harmful substance in the body, such as a virus or bacterium.

bacterium (plural: bacteria)
Bacteria are very simple, microscopic living creatures that cause decay or infection in plants and animals.

biological weapon
A weapon that kills or injures by spreading deadly germs or poisons.

cell
The smallest, most basic structure of a living thing.

contaminated
Spoiled, polluted, or dirty.

diarrhea
A health problem in which the gut contents become more liquid and move more quickly through the body.

electron
The tiniest of the particles inside atoms. Atoms are the specks of material from which every object is made.

epidemic
A serious outbreak of a disease that infects many of the people in the region where it strikes.

fever
A higher body temperature than normal, often resulting in heavy sweating and uncontrollable shivering.

flea
A tiny, jumping insect without wings that feeds on human or animal blood.

germ
Something other than a poison that causes disease or bad health: a protist, virus, or bacterium.

immune
Unable to catch a disease.

infection
An invasion of the body by a germ, or the passing on of a disease from a sick person to a healthy person.

inoculation
The method of protecting against a disease by deliberately infecting healthy people with a weakened form of it.

microbe
This is basically just a fancy name for a germ.

migration
Movement of people between countries or continents.

mold
A type of tiny fungus that forms a fur-like growth on rotting plant or animal material.

mosquito
A tiny, flying, biting insect.

pandemic
A serious outbreak of a disease, affecting several continents or the world.

parasite
A plant or animal that lives and feeds on another plant or animal—without helping it or killing it.

plague
A disease that spreads quickly and kills many people in a short time.

pollution
Spoiling—often of the air, water, or soil.

prejudice
The dislike or unfair treatment of people because of their race, religion, sex, or social class.

protist
A tiny, simple living creature, often made up of just one cell.

resistance
The natural ability to fight off a disease or infection.

sewage
Liquid and solid human waste from toilets and dirty water from washing.

strain
An individual variety or type: bird flu and swine flu are both strains of influenza.

symptom
An outward sign of a disease, such as a fever, headache, or skin rash.

syringe
A tube tipped with a fine, sharp needle, used to inject drugs into the body.

vaccine
A deliberately weakened form of a disease that, when injected or swallowed into the body, gives protection against the disease.

veins (and arteries)
A network of fine tubes in the body through which blood flows back to (and away from) the heart, which pumps it around the body again.

virus
A microscopic, lifeless germ that tricks the body into copying it, until there is enough of the virus for it to become dangerous.

INDEX

A
animals 4, 9, 11, 14, 30, 35, 40
anthrax 25
antibiotics 12, 17, 41, 43
antibodies 32, 33

B
bacteria 5, 6, 7, 9, 10, 12, 25, 37, 41
biological warfare 41
bird flu 35
Black Death 11, 14–17
BSE ("mad-cow" disease) 40
bubonic plague 4, 5, 11, 14–17

C
cells 5, 7, 26, 32
childhood diseases 28–29
cholera 9, 20, 22–23, 25
Cohn, Ferdinand 25
contagion 21
coronavirus
    (COVID-19) 11, 13, 41
cowpox 33

D
dengue fever 13
diphtheria 29
drug resistance 27, 41, 43

E
E. coli 37
epidemics 12, 13, 19, 21, 22, 31, 33, 39
    ergotism 38–39

F
flu (influenza) 11, 34–35
food poisoning 37
fungus 38–39

G
germ theory 24–25
germ types 5
German measles 29

H
HIV 11, 13
Hong Kong flu 11
humours, theory of 20–21

IJ
immune system 10, 32, 33, 35
immunity 28, 29, 35
immunization 32, 33
infections 8, 9, 10
inoculation 31
insect-borne diseases 12, 13, 26–27
Jenner, Edward 33

KL
Koch, Robert 25
leprosy 8, 18–19

M
malaria 5, 26–27
measles 28, 29
miasmas 20, 22
microbiology 25
microscopes 6–7
mumps 29

OP
Onesimus 31
pandemics 10–11, 14–17, 34, 35
parasites 26
Pasteur, Louis 24
pasteurization 24, 25
plant diseases 36–37
polio 13
pollution 9, 22, 23
potato blight 36
protists 5, 7, 13, 26, 27

Q
quarantine 15

S
salmonella 37
SARS (severe acute respiratory syndrome) 40
scarlet fever 29
sin and punishment 17, 18, 21

smallpox ...
smallpox 5, 11, 30–31, 33
Snow, John 22
Spanish flu 34
spread of disease 8–9, 10
symptoms 8, 9

T
theories of disease 20–21, 24–25
tuberculosis 19, 25, 42–43
typhoid 12
typhus 12, 36

V
vaccines 12, 13, 25, 29, 30, 33, 35, 43
viruses 5, 7, 10, 12, 13, 31, 34, 35

W
whooping cough 29

X
X-rays 42

Y
yellow fever 12

PICTURE CREDITS
The Publisher would like to thank the following for permission to reproduce their material. Every care has been taken to trace copyright holders. However, if there have been unintentional omissions or failure to trace copyright holders, we apologise and will, if informed, endeavour to make corrections in any future edition.
(t = top, b = bottom, c = center, r = right, l = left):
Pages 5tl Science Photo Library (SPL); 5tl SPL/Barry Dowsett; 5tr SPL/D. Ferguson/ISM; 5tc SPL/Eye of Science; 6b Shutterstock/ Irina Tischenko; 7t Alamy/History and Art Collection; 7c SPL/Eye of Science; 7br SPL/ Steve Allen; 13tr Shutterstock/Photomay; 13b Shutterstock/Biomedical; 18 Professor Shimon Gibson; 19tr SPL/Meckes/Otawa; 19cl SPL/Dr Kari Lounatmaa; 19cr SPL/ Ajay Verma; 20 Shutterstock/Tomas Palsovic; 23tl SPL/IML; 23bl SPL/IML; 23c SPL/CCI Archives; 23br Getty/ Hulton Archive; 24 AKG/
Musée d'Orsay; 25t SPL/James King-Holmes; 25c iStock/ Grafissimo; 25r AKG/Archiv für Kunst & Geschichte, Berlin; 27c Shutterstock/leospek; 27r Shutterstock, 28 Shutterstock/phichet chaiyabin; 31c Shutterstock/DuxX; 31bl Getty/Science & Society Picture Library; 31bc Getty/ Images; 32 SPL; 33b Getty/Bettmann; 33c iStockphoto; 34b Shutterstock/pcruciatti; 34tl Shutterstock/Heritage 35 Shutterstock/pcruciatti; 36 Getty/Hulton Archive; 37tr Shutterstock/Sebastian Kaulitzki; 37cr Shutterstock/ Michael Taylor; 37b Alamy/Nigel Cattlin; 39l Shutterstock/ Images; 39r Shutterstock/Everett Historical; 40 Alamy/Arco Mikhal Malyshev; 41 Getty/Yuri Smityuk; 42 Shutterstock/ Puwadol Jaturawutthichai; 43 Shutterstock/Julia Sanders; 45c Getty/J. Carrier; 45br Peter Shutterstock/Chatchai.wa; 45b Probst/Alamy Stock Photo.